THE Breakup BAND AID Workbook

Sarah Melland

DEDICATED TO YOU

This book is for you. The ones who love to write, the ones who hate to write, and the ones that get the job done by writing.

CONTENTS

STEP 1:
Admit You Are Powerless Over Your Ex

What have you done so far that has made you hit rock bottom? Journal all of your mishaps. Don't be ashamed, know we all have been there. It is OK to cry during this time. Write down everything so you never ever, and I mean ever, repeat this in your next breakup.

_____

_____

_____

_____

_____

_____

_____

_____

_____

_____

_____

_____

_____

_____

_____

_____

_____

_____

_____

_____

_____

_____

_____

_____

_____

_____

_____

_____

_____

STEP 2:
Get Rid of Everything Reminding you of your ex

Make a list of everything you have that reminds you of your ex, and I mean everything! Get rid of it. I am telling you to say goodbye to that junk. It is pure and utter junk.

You can also use this as a money-making list. If your ex bought you expensive gifts and you want to sell them, mark on here how much and when you sold it.

❖ _____

❖ _____

❖ _____

❖ _____

❖ _____

❖ _____

❖ _____

❖ _____

❖ _____

❖ _____

❖ _____

❖ _____

❖
❖
❖
❖
❖
❖
❖
❖
❖
❖
❖
❖
❖
❖
❖
❖
❖
❖

_____
_____
_____
_____
_____
_____
_____
_____
_____
_____
_____
_____
_____
_____
_____
_____
_____
_____

❖ _____

❖ _____

❖ _____

❖ _____

❖ _____

❖ _____

❖ _____

❖ _____

❖ _____

❖ _____

❖ _____

❖ _____

❖ _____

❖ _____

❖ _____

❖ _____

❖ _____

❖ _____

❖ _____

STEP 3:
Get a Sponsor.
We Know You're a Trainwreck

This is for writing down who is going to help you through this difficult time. Also, write down ideas for how you are going to pay your sponsor back. Maybe even journal how they were able to stop you from being a menace to yourself or your ex.

_____

_____

_____

_____

_____

_____

_____

_____

_____

_____

_____

_____

_____

_____

_____

_____

_____

_____

_____

_____

_____

_____

_____

_____

_____

_____

_____

_____

_____

_____

_____

_____

_____

_____

_____

_____

_____

_____

_____

_____

_____

_____

_____

_____

_____

_____

_____

_____

STEP 4:
List What a Spectacular Catch You Are

List everything you love about yourself, even down to your finger nails. I don't care if you think you don't have good qualities. You absolutely do! Write down your laugh. Write down your smile. Those are always, no matter what anyone tells you, beautiful!

❖ _____

❖ _____

❖ _____

❖ _____

❖ _____

❖ _____

❖ _____

❖ _____

❖ _____

❖ _____

❖ _____

❖ _____

❖ _____

❖ _____

❖ _____

❖ _____

❖ _____

❖ _____

❖ _____

❖ _____

❖ _____

❖ _____

❖ _____

❖ _____

❖ _____

❖ _____

❖ _____

❖ _____

❖ _____

❖ _____

❖ _____

❖ _____

❖ _____

❖ _____

STEP 5:
Admit Your Faults in The Relationship

Again, this is just to help you so you don't do the same things wrong in your next relationship. This is a learning tool.

❖ _____

_____

_____

_____

❖ _____

_____

_____

_____

❖ _____

_____

_____

❖ _____

_____

❖ _____

_____

_____

_____

❖ _____

_____

_____

_____

❖ _____

_____

_____

_____

❖ _____

_____

_____

_____

STEP 6:
Don't Contact or Stalk Your Ex
For 60 Days

Please document your struggles and what you are trying to work through these next 60 days. Also, write down what you decided to do instead of stalking their social media. You will be surprised at how much you can accomplish during a day, once you stop stalking.

DAY 1 _____

_____

DAY 2 _____

_____

DAY 3 _____

_____

DAY 4 _____

_____

DAY 5 _____

DAY 6 _____

_____

DAY 7 _____

_____

DAY 8 _____

_____

DAY 9 _____

_____

DAY 10 _____

_____

DAY 11 _____

_____

DAY 12 _____

_____

DAY 13 _____

_____

DAY 14 _____

_____

DAY 15 _____

_____

DAY 16 _____

_____

DAY 17 _____

_____

DAY 18 _____

_____

DAY 19 _____

_____

DAY 20 _____

_____

DAY 21 _____

_____

DAY 22 _____

_____

DAY 23 _____

_____

DAY 24 _____

_____

DAY 25 _____

_____

DAY 26 _____

_____

DAY 27 _____

_____

DAY 28 _____

_____

DAY 29 _____

_____

DAY 30 _____

_____

This should be getting easier by now.

DAY 31 _____

DAY 32 _____

DAY 33 _____

DAY 34 _____

DAY 35 _____

DAY 36 _____

DAY 37 _____

DAY 38 _____

DAY 39 _____

DAY 40 _____

DAY 41 _____

DAY 42 _____

DAY 43 _____

DAY 44 _____

DAY 45 _____

DAY 46 _____

DAY 47 _____

DAY 48 _____

DAY 49 _____

DAY 50 _____

You are on the home stretch. You're doing great!

DAY 51 _____

DAY 52 _____

DAY 53 _____

DAY 54 _____

DAY 55 _____

DAY 56 _____

DAY 57 _____

DAY 58 _____

DAY 59 _____

DAY 60 _____

Don't you dare think because you completed this step, it is OK to stalk now. It is absolutely not!

STEP 7:
Quit Your Bad Habits

List all of your bad habits you need to quit before your next relationship. This isn't bad habits in the relationship, this is bad habits in general. Do you smoke? Do you drink too much? Are you a hermit? Do you collect toenail clippings? Acknowledging your bad habits on paper will help you see how ridiculous they are and that they get to stop now!

❖ _____

❖ _____

❖ _____

❖ _____

❖ _____

❖ _____

❖ _____

❖ _____

❖ _____

❖ _____

❖ _____

❖ _____

❖ _____

STEP 8:
List People You Have Harmed While Being a Trainwreck

Did you bite your friend when they tried to take your phone away? Write their name down.

❖ _____

❖ _____

❖ _____

❖ _____

❖ _____

❖ _____

❖ _____

❖ _____

❖ _____

❖ _____

❖ _____

❖ _____

❖ _____

❖ _____

❖ _____

STEP 9:
Apologize to Them

Now you get to apologize to all of them. How exciting! I am supplying you dates and times to meet up. Also, a check box so you can cross their name off when you apologize.

☐ _____ / __ / __

☐ _____ / __ / __

☐ _____ / __ / __

☐ _____ / __ / __

☐ _____ / __ / __

☐ _____ / __ / __

☐ _____ / __ / __

☐ _____ / __ / __

☐ _____ / __ / __

☐ _____ / __ / __

☐ _____ / __ / __

☐ _____ / __ / __

☐ _____ / __ / __

☐ _____ / __ / __

☐ _____ / __ / __

☐ _____ / __ / __

STEP 10:
No One Likes a Backslider

Write a love letter to yourself for the next seven days. Here is a sample one I wrote. If you want to, for the first day, you can absolutely copy it. After the seven days, read them out loud to yourself. It might sound stupid, but it really helps. Trust me!

My Beautiful Sarah,

I miss the way your adorning smile shines down from the clouds above. Your effervescent beauty reigns from within. How I wish I could give you everything and more. I never want to see you sad. You deserve the respect and cherishment I am willing to give you.

How I have missed you for far too long. I miss your laugh, I miss your wit, your intelligent conversations. I miss the way you would listen to me, and your utmost compassion. You bring a peace to me I never thought was possible.

I hope this finds you well and in good spirits my darling love, and know that I will always be with you.

Love Always,

Sarah Marie

Dear _____,

_____

_____

_____

_____

_____

_____

_____

_____

_____

_____

_____

_____

_____

_____

_____

_____

_____

_____

_____

_____

_____

Love Always,

_____

My Amazing_____,

_____

_____

_____

_____

_____

_____

_____

_____

_____

_____

_____

_____

_____

_____

_____

_____

_____

_____

_____

Love Always,

_____

My Talented_____**,**

_____

_____

_____

_____

_____

_____

_____

_____

_____

_____

_____

_____

_____

_____

_____

_____

_____

_____

_____

_____

_____

Love Always,

_____

My Caring_____,

_____

_____

_____

_____

_____

_____

_____

_____

_____

_____

_____

_____

_____

_____

_____

_____

_____

_____

_____

_____

Love Always,

_____

My Loving_____**,**

_____

_____

_____

_____

_____

_____

_____

_____

_____

_____

_____

_____

_____

_____

_____

_____

_____

_____

_____

_____

Love Always,

_____

My Beautiful_____,

_____

_____

_____

_____

_____

_____

_____

_____

_____

_____

_____

_____

_____

_____

_____

_____

_____

_____

_____

_____

_____

Love Always,

_____

My Authentic_____,

_____

_____

_____

_____

_____

_____

_____

_____

_____

_____

_____

_____

_____

_____

_____

_____

_____

_____

_____

Love Always,

_____

STEP 11:
Last-Ditch Effort

You can write down any last-ditch attempts you want to try. Take notes and research what other types of therapy or classes might be helpful here.

_____

_____

_____

_____

_____

_____

_____

_____

_____

_____

_____

_____

STEP 12:
Wake Up and Smell the Coffee

What are your goals today? How will you improve this life for yourself and others? What is one little thing you could do today that would accomplish this feat? Again, I know you love making lists, so I will put this section in list form. As always, you are welcome!

❖ _____

❖ _____

❖ _____

❖ _____

❖ _____

❖ _____

❖ _____

❖ _____

❖ _____

❖ _____

❖ _____

❖ _____

❖ _____

❖ _____

❖ _____

❖ _____

❖ _____

❖ _____

❖ _____

❖ _____

❖ _____

❖ _____

❖ _____

❖ _____

❖ _____

❖ _____

❖ _____

❖ _____

❖ _____

❖ _____

❖ _____

❖ _____

❖ _____

DO THESE INSTEAD

When you are feeling frisky, write down all the things you have always wanted to try. These will have a checkbox so you can check these accomplishments off when you do them. I am so excited that you are going out and trying new things.

ACTIVITIES

☐ _____

☐ _____

☐ _____

☐ _____

☐ _____

☐ _____

☐ _____

☐ _____

☐ _____

☐ _____

☐ _____

☐ _____

☐ _____

ATTRACTIONS

☐ _____
☐ _____
☐ _____
☐ _____
☐ _____
☐ _____
☐ _____
☐ _____
☐ _____
☐ _____
☐ _____
☐ _____
☐ _____
☐ _____
☐ _____
☐ _____
☐ _____
☐ _____

HOBBIES

- [ ] _____
- [ ] _____
- [ ] _____
- [ ] _____
- [ ] _____
- [ ] _____
- [ ] _____
- [ ] _____
- [ ] _____
- [ ] _____
- [ ] _____
- [ ] _____
- [ ] _____
- [ ] _____
- [ ] _____
- [ ] _____
- [ ] _____
- [ ] _____

CLASSES

- ☐ _____
- ☐ _____
- ☐ _____
- ☐ _____
- ☐ _____
- ☐ _____
- ☐ _____
- ☐ _____
- ☐ _____
- ☐ _____
- ☐ _____
- ☐ _____
- ☐ _____
- ☐ _____
- ☐ _____
- ☐ _____
- ☐ _____
- ☐ _____

PAMPERING

☐ _____

☐ _____

☐ _____

☐ _____

☐ _____

☐ _____

☐ _____

☐ _____

☐ _____

☐ _____

☐ _____

☐ _____

☐ _____

☐ _____

☐ _____

☐ _____

☐ _____

☐ _____

HEALTH

☐ _____

☐ _____

☐ _____

☐ _____

☐ _____

☐ _____

☐ _____

☐ _____

☐ _____

☐ _____

☐ _____

☐ _____

☐ _____

☐ _____

☐ _____

☐ _____

☐ _____

☐ _____

FITNESS

☐ _____

☐ _____

☐ _____

☐ _____

☐ _____

☐ _____

☐ _____

☐ _____

☐ _____

☐ _____

☐ _____

☐ _____

☐ _____

☐ _____

☐ _____

☐ _____

☐ _____

STAY AT HOME IDEAS

- [ ] _____
- [ ] _____
- [ ] _____
- [ ] _____
- [ ] _____
- [ ] _____
- [ ] _____
- [ ] _____
- [ ] _____
- [ ] _____
- [ ] _____
- [ ] _____
- [ ] _____
- [ ] _____
- [ ] _____
- [ ] _____
- [ ] _____
- [ ] _____

SCHOOL IDEAS

☐ _____

☐ _____

☐ _____

☐ _____

☐ _____

☐ _____

☐ _____

☐ _____

☐ _____

☐ _____

☐ _____

☐ _____

☐ _____

☐ _____

☐ _____

☐ _____

☐ _____

☐ _____

WORK IDEAS

☐ _____
☐ _____
☐ _____
☐ _____
☐ _____
☐ _____
☐ _____
☐ _____
☐ _____
☐ _____
☐ _____
☐ _____
☐ _____
☐ _____
☐ _____
☐ _____
☐ _____
☐ _____

MISCELLANOUS

☐ _____

☐ _____

☐ _____

☐ _____

☐ _____

☐ _____

☐ _____

☐ _____

☐ _____

☐ _____

☐ _____

☐ _____

☐ _____

☐ _____

☐ _____

☐ _____

☐ _____

☐ _____

TRAVEL BUCKET LIST

Here is a make-your-own bucket list. I know you wanted one after reading *The Breakup Band Aid*. Plus, I gave you some extra room for jotting down notes on where to stay, travel deals, and when to go. Look up sites such as travelzoo.com for all-inclusive cheap deals. There are a ton of blogs, as well, which tell you how to save money, travel tips and the best time to go.

NORTH AMERICA

❑ _____

❑ _____

❑ _____

❑ _____

❑ _____

❑ _____

❑ _____

❑ _____

❑ _____

❑ _____

❑ _____

❑ _____

❑ _____

❑ _____

❑ _____

- ☐ _____
- ☐ _____
- ☐ _____
- ☐ _____
- ☐ _____
- ☐ _____
- ☐ _____
- ☐ _____
- ☐ _____
- ☐ _____
- ☐ _____
- ☐ _____
- ☐ _____
- ☐ _____
- ☐ _____
- ☐ _____
- ☐ _____
- ☐ _____
- ☐ _____
- ☐ _____
- ☐ _____
- ☐ _____
- ☐ _____
- ☐ _____

WHERE TO STAY

❖ _____ $/night _____

❖ _____ $/night _____

❖ _____ $/night _____

❖ _____ $/night _____

❖ _____ $/night _____

❖ _____ $/night _____

❖ _____ $/night _____

❖ _____ $/night _____

❖ _____ $/night _____

❖ _____ $/night _____

TRAVEL DEALS

_____

_____

_____

_____

_____

_____

_____

_____

_____

_____

WHEN TO GO

_____

_____

_____

_____

_____

_____

_____

_____

OTHER

_____

_____

_____

_____

_____

_____

_____

_____

_____

SOUTH AMERICA

- [ ] _____
- [ ] _____
- [ ] _____
- [ ] _____
- [ ] _____
- [ ] _____
- [ ] _____
- [ ] _____
- [ ] _____
- [ ] _____
- [ ] _____
- [ ] _____
- [ ] _____
- [ ] _____
- [ ] _____
- [ ] _____
- [ ] _____
- [ ] _____
- [ ] _____
- [ ] _____
- [ ] _____
- [ ] _____
- [ ] _____
- [ ] _____
- [ ] _____

☐ _____
☐ _____
☐ _____
☐ _____
☐ _____
☐ _____
☐ _____
☐ _____
☐ _____
☐ _____
☐ _____
☐ _____
☐ _____
☐ _____
☐ _____
☐ _____
☐ _____
☐ _____
☐ _____
☐ _____
☐ _____
☐ _____
☐ _____
☐ _____

WHERE TO STAY

❖ _____ $/night _____

❖ _____ $/night _____

❖ _____ $/night _____

❖ _____ $/night _____

❖ _____ $/night _____

❖ _____ $/night _____

❖ _____ $/night _____

❖ _____ $/night _____

❖ _____ $/night _____

❖ _____ $/night _____

TRAVEL DEALS

_____

_____

_____

_____

_____

_____

_____

_____

_____

_____

WHEN TO GO

_____

_____

_____

_____

_____

_____

_____

_____

_____

OTHER

_____

_____

_____

_____

_____

_____

_____

_____

_____

_____

AFRICA

- [ ] _____
- [ ] _____
- [ ] _____
- [ ] _____
- [ ] _____
- [ ] _____
- [ ] _____
- [ ] _____
- [ ] _____
- [ ] _____
- [ ] _____
- [ ] _____
- [ ] _____
- [ ] _____
- [ ] _____
- [ ] _____
- [ ] _____
- [ ] _____
- [ ] _____
- [ ] _____
- [ ] _____
- [ ] _____
- [ ] _____
- [ ] _____

- ☐ _____
- ☐ _____
- ☐ _____
- ☐ _____
- ☐ _____
- ☐ _____
- ☐ _____
- ☐ _____
- ☐ _____
- ☐ _____
- ☐ _____
- ☐ _____
- ☐ _____
- ☐ _____
- ☐ _____
- ☐ _____
- ☐ _____
- ☐ _____
- ☐ _____
- ☐ _____
- ☐ _____
- ☐ _____
- ☐ _____
- ☐ _____
- ☐ _____

WHERE TO STAY

❖ _____ $/night _____

❖ _____ $/night _____

❖ _____ $/night _____

❖ _____ $/night _____

❖ _____ $/night _____

❖ _____ $/night _____

❖ _____ $/night _____

❖ _____ $/night _____

❖ _____ $/night _____

❖ _____ $/night _____

TRAVEL DEALS

_____

_____

_____

_____

_____

_____

_____

_____

_____

_____

WHEN TO GO

OTHER

EUROPE

- ☐ _____
- ☐ _____
- ☐ _____
- ☐ _____
- ☐ _____
- ☐ _____
- ☐ _____
- ☐ _____
- ☐ _____
- ☐ _____
- ☐ _____
- ☐ _____
- ☐ _____
- ☐ _____
- ☐ _____
- ☐ _____
- ☐ _____
- ☐ _____
- ☐ _____
- ☐ _____
- ☐ _____
- ☐ _____
- ☐ _____
- ☐ _____
- ☐ _____

☐ _____
☐ _____
☐ _____
☐ _____
☐ _____
☐ _____
☐ _____
☐ _____
☐ _____
☐ _____
☐ _____
☐ _____
☐ _____
☐ _____
☐ _____
☐ _____
☐ _____
☐ _____
☐ _____
☐ _____
☐ _____
☐ _____
☐ _____
☐ _____
☐ _____
☐ _____

WHERE TO STAY

❖ _____ $/night _____

❖ _____ $/night _____

❖ _____ $/night _____

❖ _____ $/night _____

❖ _____ $/night _____

❖ _____ $/night _____

❖ _____ $/night _____

❖ _____ $/night _____

❖ _____ $/night _____

❖ _____ $/night _____

TRAVEL DEALS

_____

_____

_____

_____

_____

_____

_____

_____

_____

_____

WHEN TO GO

_____

_____

_____

_____

_____

_____

_____

_____

_____

OTHER

_____

_____

_____

_____

_____

_____

_____

_____

_____

ASIA

- ☐ _____
- ☐ _____
- ☐ _____
- ☐ _____
- ☐ _____
- ☐ _____
- ☐ _____
- ☐ _____
- ☐ _____
- ☐ _____
- ☐ _____
- ☐ _____
- ☐ _____
- ☐ _____
- ☐ _____
- ☐ _____
- ☐ _____
- ☐ _____
- ☐ _____
- ☐ _____
- ☐ _____
- ☐ _____
- ☐ _____
- ☐ _____

- ☐ _____
- ☐ _____
- ☐ _____
- ☐ _____
- ☐ _____
- ☐ _____
- ☐ _____
- ☐ _____
- ☐ _____
- ☐ _____
- ☐ _____
- ☐ _____
- ☐ _____
- ☐ _____
- ☐ _____
- ☐ _____
- ☐ _____
- ☐ _____
- ☐ _____
- ☐ _____
- ☐ _____
- ☐ _____
- ☐ _____
- ☐ _____
- ☐ _____

WHERE TO STAY

❖ _____ $/night _____

❖ _____ $/night _____

❖ _____ $/night _____

❖ _____ $/night _____

❖ _____ $/night _____

❖ _____ $/night _____

❖ _____ $/night _____

❖ _____ $/night _____

❖ _____ $/night _____

❖ _____ $/night _____

TRAVEL DEALS

_____

_____

_____

_____

_____

_____

_____

_____

_____

_____

WHEN TO GO

_____
_____
_____
_____
_____
_____
_____
_____
_____

OTHER

_____
_____
_____
_____
_____
_____
_____
_____
_____

AUSTRALIA

☐ _____
☐ _____
☐ _____
☐ _____
☐ _____
☐ _____
☐ _____
☐ _____
☐ _____
☐ _____
☐ _____
☐ _____
☐ _____
☐ _____
☐ _____
☐ _____
☐ _____
☐ _____
☐ _____
☐ _____
☐ _____
☐ _____
☐ _____

WHERE TO STAY

❖ _____ $/night _____

❖ _____ $/night _____

❖ _____ $/night _____

❖ _____ $/night _____

❖ _____ $/night _____

❖ _____ $/night _____

❖ _____ $/night _____

❖ _____ $/night _____

❖ _____ $/night _____

❖ _____ $/night _____

TRAVEL DEALS

_____

_____

_____

_____

_____

_____

_____

_____

_____

_____

WHEN TO GO

_____
_____
_____
_____
_____
_____
_____
_____
_____
_____

OTHER

_____
_____
_____
_____
_____
_____
_____
_____
_____
_____

BOOKS TO READ

This can be self-help books, classics, or humor. Whatever you want to put in. You can even get friends together and start a book club once a month with wine and appetizers. Culture yourself.

- ☐ _____
- ☐ _____
- ☐ _____
- ☐ _____
- ☐ _____
- ☐ _____
- ☐ _____
- ☐ _____
- ☐ _____
- ☐ _____
- ☐ _____
- ☐ _____
- ☐ _____
- ☐ _____
- ☐ _____
- ☐ _____
- ☐ _____
- ☐ _____
- ☐ _____
- ☐ _____

- [ ]
- [ ]
- [ ]
- [ ]
- [ ]
- [ ]
- [ ]
- [ ]
- [ ]
- [ ]
- [ ]
- [ ]
- [ ]
- [ ]
- [ ]
- [ ]
- [ ]
- [ ]
- [ ]
- [ ]
- [ ]
- [ ]
- [ ]
- [ ]
- [ ]
- [ ]

MOVIES TO WATCH

If you never got around to watching a specific genre of movies, because your ex hated those kinds of movies, write them down. Now, you can watch all you want.

- ❑ _____
- ❑ _____
- ❑ _____
- ❑ _____
- ❑ _____
- ❑ _____
- ❑ _____
- ❑ _____
- ❑ _____
- ❑ _____
- ❑ _____
- ❑ _____
- ❑ _____
- ❑ _____
- ❑ _____
- ❑ _____
- ❑ _____
- ❑ _____
- ❑ _____
- ❑ _____
- ❑ _____

SARAH MELLAND

- ☐ _____
- ☐ _____
- ☐ _____
- ☐ _____
- ☐ _____
- ☐ _____
- ☐ _____
- ☐ _____
- ☐ _____
- ☐ _____
- ☐ _____
- ☐ _____
- ☐ _____
- ☐ _____
- ☐ _____
- ☐ _____
- ☐ _____
- ☐ _____
- ☐ _____
- ☐ _____
- ☐ _____
- ☐ _____
- ☐ _____
- ☐ _____

EMPOWERING QUOTES TO LIVE BY

Any and all inspirational, empowering, and motivational quotes you want to live by. Whenever you come across one, just write it down. Read them from time to time to remember you are flipping, awesomely insane!

_____

_____

_____

By:_____

_____

_____

_____

By:_____

_____

_____

_____

By:_____

_____

_____

_____

By:_____

_____

_____

_____

By:_____

_____

_____

_____

By:_____

_____

_____

_____

By:_____

_____

_____

_____

By:_____

_____

_____

_____

By:_____

_____

_____

_____

By:_____

_____

_____

_____

By:_____

FOOD JOURNAL

Here is a seven-day jump start food diary to help you feel like a new you. Sometimes people like to journal what they eat in a day, or just to have a meal plan in place. Maybe jot down some recipes you want to try. Anything and everything goes.

DAY 1

Breakfast

_____

_____

Snack

_____

Lunch

_____

_____

Snack

_____

Dinner

_____

_____

DAY 2

Breakfast

_____

_____

_____

Snack

_____

Lunch

_____

_____

_____

Snack

_____

Dinner

_____

_____

_____

DAY 3

Breakfast

_____

_____

_____

Snack

_____

Lunch

_____

_____

_____

Snack

_____

Dinner

_____

_____

_____

DAY 4

Breakfast

_____

_____

_____

Snack

_____

Lunch

_____

_____

_____

Snack

_____

Dinner

_____

_____

_____

DAY 5

Breakfast

_____

_____

_____

Snack

_____

Lunch

_____

_____

_____

Snack

_____

Dinner

_____

_____

_____

DAY 6

Breakfast

_____
_____
_____

Snack

_____

Lunch

_____
_____
_____

Snack

_____

Dinner

_____
_____
_____

DAY 7

Breakfast

_____

_____

_____

Snack

_____

Lunch

_____

_____

_____

Snack

_____

Dinner

_____

_____

_____

Recipe

_____
_____
_____
_____
_____
_____
_____
_____
_____
_____

Recipe

_____
_____
_____
_____
_____
_____
_____
_____
_____
_____

Recipe

_____

_____

_____

_____

_____

_____

_____

_____

_____

Recipe

_____

_____

_____

_____

_____

_____

_____

_____

_____

Recipe

_____
_____
_____
_____
_____
_____
_____
_____
_____
_____

Recipe

_____
_____
_____
_____
_____
_____
_____
_____
_____
_____

Helpful Tips

❖ _____

❖ _____

❖ _____

❖ _____

❖ _____

❖ _____

❖ _____

❖ _____

❖ _____

❖ _____

❖ _____

❖ _____

❖ _____

❖ _____

❖ _____

❖ _____

❖ _____

❖ _____

❖ _____

❖ _____

❖ _____

❖

Notes

A LIST OF WHY YOUR EX SUCKED

This is the breakup list of all breakup lists. The reason Ross and Rachel broke up. The reason why I probably never got over my ex, because I didn't make one. Do yourself a favor and make one.

❖ _____
❖ _____
❖ _____
❖ _____
❖ _____
❖ _____
❖ _____
❖ _____
❖ _____
❖ _____
❖ _____
❖ _____
❖ _____
❖ _____
❖ _____
❖ _____
❖ _____
❖ _____
❖ _____

❖ _____
❖ _____
❖ _____
❖ _____
❖ _____
❖ _____
❖ _____
❖ _____
❖ _____
❖ _____
❖ _____
❖ _____
❖ _____
❖ _____
❖ _____
❖ _____
❖ _____
❖ _____
❖ _____
❖ _____
❖ _____
❖ _____
❖ _____

QUALITIES YOU WANT IN A PARTNER

Anything and everything you have ever wanted in a partner goes on this list. If it's down on paper, you can manifest it. Come back sometimes and add to it. This is what you WANT in a partner. NOT what you DON'T WANT. Remember that.

❖ _____
❖ _____
❖ _____
❖ _____
❖ _____
❖ _____
❖ _____
❖ _____
❖ _____
❖ _____
❖ _____
❖ _____
❖ _____
❖ _____
❖ _____
❖ _____
❖ _____
❖ _____

❖ _____
❖ _____
❖ _____
❖ _____
❖ _____
❖ _____
❖ _____
❖ _____
❖ _____
❖ _____
❖ _____
❖ _____
❖ _____
❖ _____
❖ _____
❖ _____
❖ _____
❖ _____
❖ _____
❖ _____
❖ _____
❖ _____
❖ _____

JOURNALING THROUGH THE PAIN

Write down the moments in your relationship that hurt you the most. Remember the pain and why you would never want to go through that again with another significant other.

_____

_____

_____

_____

_____

_____

_____

_____

_____

_____

_____

_____

_____

_____

_____

_____

_____

_____

_____

_____

_____

_____

_____

_____

_____

_____

_____

_____

_____

_____

_____

_____

_____

_____

_____

_____

_____

_____

_____

_____

_____

_____

_____

_____

_____

_____

_____

_____

_____

_____

_____

_____

_____

_____

_____

_____

_____

_____

_____

_____

_____

_____

_____

_____

_____

_____

_____

_____

_____

JOURNALING TO TRIUMPH

Make a record of your progress. The beautiful things you have come in contact with. The marvelous adventures you have been on. The new hobbies you have tried. Write down all of your accomplishments this past year. Everything that you are proud of.

_____

_____

_____

_____

_____

_____

_____

_____

_____

_____

_____

_____

_____

_____

_____

_____

_____

_____

_____

_____

_____

_____

_____

_____

_____

_____

_____

_____

_____

_____

_____

_____

_____

_____

_____

_____

_____

_____

_____

_____

_____

_____

_____

_____

_____

_____

_____

_____

_____

_____

_____

_____

_____

_____

_____

_____

_____

_____

_____

_____

_____

_____

_____

_____

_____

_____

_____

_____

_____

_____

_____

_____

_____

_____

_____

_____

_____

_____

_____

_____

_____

_____

_____

_____

_____

_____

_____

_____

_____

_____

_____

_____

_____

_____

_____

_____

_____

_____

_____

_____

_____

_____

_____

_____

_____

_____

_____

OTHER NOTES TO INSPIRE

Random thoughts that pop into your head. I recommend keeping this workbook and pen near your bed at night for when you wake up and have an amazing idea so you don't forget it in the morning. As always, you are welcome.

_____

_____

_____

_____

_____

_____

_____

_____

_____

_____

_____

_____

_____

_____

_____

_____

_____

_____

_____

_____

_____

_____

_____

_____

_____

_____

_____

_____

_____

_____

_____

_____

_____

_____

_____

_____

_____

_____

_____

_____

_____

_____

_____

_____

_____

_____

_____

_____

_____

_____

_____

_____

_____

_____

_____

_____

_____

_____

_____

_____

_____

_____

_____

_____

_____

_____

_____

_____

_____

_____

_____

_____

_____

_____

_____

_____

_____

_____

_____

_____

_____

_____

_____

_____

_____

_____

_____

_____

_____

_____

_____

_____

_____

_____

_____

_____

_____

_____

_____

_____

_____

_____

_____

_____

_____

_____

_____

_____

_____

_____

_____

_____

_____

_____

_____

_____

_____

_____

_____

_____

_____

_____

_____

_____

Made in the USA
Middletown, DE
03 January 2018